The Persian Gulf War

by Andrew Santella

Content Adviser: Jack A. Green,
Persian Gulf War Veteran, Public Affairs Officer,
Naval Historical Center, Washington, D.C.

Reading Adviser: Dr. Linda D. Labbo,
Department of Reading Education, College of Education
The University of Georgia

COMPASS POINT BOOKS
MINNEAPOLIS, MINNESOTA

Compass Point Books
3109 West 50th Street, #115
Minneapolis, MN 55410

Visit Compass Point Books on the Internet at *www.compasspointbooks.com*
or e-mail your request to *custserv@compasspointbooks.com*

On the cover: U.S. Marines roll into Kuwait International Airport in light armored vehicles after the retreat of Iraqi forces during Operation Desert Storm.

Photographs ©: Defense Visual Information Center, cover, 15, 17, 23, 36; David Turnley/Corbis, 4, 5, 6, 29, 30; Getty Images, 7; Larry Lee Photography/Corbis, 8; Yann Arthus-Bertrand/Corbis, 9; Wally McNamee/Corbis, 10; Jacques Langevin/Corbis Sygma, 11, 28; Reuters NewMedia Inc./Corbis, 14, 33; Howard Davies/Corbis, 16; Patrick Durand/Corbis Sygma, 19, 22, 32; David Rubinger/Corbis, 21; Francoise de Mulder/Corbis, 25; AFP/Getty Images, 27, 34, 37, 41; AFP/Corbis, 35, 38, 39.

Editor: Catherine Neitge
Photo Researcher: Svetlana Zhurkina
Designer/Page Production: Bradfordesign, Inc./Biner Design
Cartographer: XNR Productions, Inc.

Library of Congress Cataloging-in-Publication Data
Santella, Andrew.
  The Persian Gulf War / by Andrew Santella.
    p. cm. — (We the people)
  Includes bibliographical references and index.
Contents: The fall of Kuwait—Saddam Hussein's wars—The world responds—Desert Storm—
The ground war—After the war.
  ISBN 0-7565-0612-3
  1. Persian Gulf War, 1991—Juvenile literature. [1. Persian Gulf War, 1991.] I. Title. II. Series:
We the people (Compass Point Books)
  DS79.723.S26 2004
  956.7044'2—dc22   2003014439

TABLE OF CONTENTS

NOTE: *In this book, words that are defined in the glossary are in* **bold** *the first time they appear in the text.*

THE FALL OF KUWAIT

There seemed to be no stopping Iraq's army. Early on the morning of August 2, 1990, Iraq invaded the tiny neighboring nation of Kuwait. Kuwait's border patrols had no chance to turn back the invasion. Iraq boasted the fourth-largest army in the world. About 100,000 Iraqi troops and 300 tanks rolled into Kuwait that day.

An Iraqi soldier shouts to his men as they train after the invasion of Kuwait.

4

Kuwait's army only had 18,000 soldiers ready to fight. Within a day, Iraq controlled all of Kuwait.

Iraq's invasion of Kuwait outraged much of the world. It was the first step toward what would come to be called the Persian Gulf War. The United Nations condemned Iraq's invasion and demanded that Iraq withdraw from Kuwait. Eventually, the United States and 38 other nations banded together to drive the Iraqis out of Kuwait.

The war that resulted was a quick one. Some have called the Persian Gulf War the Hundred Hours War because it featured just four days of on-the-ground combat. Even though the war itself was short, its impact would be felt for years to come.

American soldiers march in formation in Saudi Arabia as they prepare to liberate Kuwait.

SADDAM HUSSEIN'S WARS

Iraq's invasion of Kuwait was ordered by Iraqi president

Saddam Hussein. Since becoming Iraq's leader in 1979, Hussein had done all he could to expand Iraq's power. Iraq's vast supplies of valuable oil should have made the country very wealthy. However, Hussein used that oil money to build and equip Iraq's huge army. He also hoped to build nuclear weapons and other weapons of mass destruction.

A poster of Saddam Hussein hangs behind Iraqi soldiers in Baghdad in 1991.

6

An Iraqi road was bombed by the Iranians during the eight-year war.

Iraq's military power helped Hussein to rule his country as a cruel **dictator.** He used his army to mistreat his own people and frighten political opponents. In 1980, he launched a war with Iraq's neighbor to the east, Iran. The war dragged on for eight years. To pay for his costly war with Iran, Hussein borrowed huge sums of money from neighboring Arab nations. One of those nations was Kuwait. By the end of the war, Iraq owed other countries more than $50 billion.

7

Kuwait was one of the wealthiest countries in the world. Like Iraq, it was rich in oil. Hussein blamed Kuwait for his economic troubles. He claimed that Kuwait was driving down the price of oil by selling oil too cheaply.

Oil refineries in Kuwait

Hussein said this was costing Iraq billions of dollars. He also claimed that Kuwait was pumping oil that belonged to Iraq. This was not the first time the two countries had argued about their shared border. Ever since Kuwait had become an independent country in 1961, Iraq had

8

claimed parts of Kuwaiti territory. Finally, in July 1990, Hussein began to threaten war with Kuwait.

On August 2, 1990, his army invaded Kuwait. Residents of Kuwait City woke that morning to find Iraqi tanks in the streets. Jaber al-Ahmad al Sabah, the emir, or leader, of Kuwait, escaped the country. Saddam Hussein annexed Kuwait, and proclaimed it part of Iraq. Hussein was now in control of much of the world's supply of oil.

Kuwait City is the capital of Kuwait

THE WORLD RESPONDS

The United Nations Security Council condemned Iraq's action. It demanded that Iraqi forces leave Kuwait immediately. Instead, Saddam Hussein sent more troops into Kuwait. Some world leaders feared that the Iraqi military action might not be finished. Iraqi troops were gathering for what appeared to be another invasion, this time of eastern Saudi Arabia.

U.S. President George H. W. Bush declared that Saddam Hussein and his army had to be stopped. "This will not stand, this aggression against Kuwait," he vowed. Bush promised to keep the Iraqis out of Saudi

President George H.W. Bush promised to get the Iraqis out of Kuwait.

10

Arabia and to push them out of Kuwait. Bush sent Defense Secretary Dick Cheney to meet with Saudi Arabia's King Fahd. They worked out a plan to send more than 200,000 American troops to Saudi Arabia to defend it against Iraq.

On August 7, U.S. troops began heading for Saudi Arabia. They were soon joined by forces from Great Britain, France, and Egypt. Before long, a **coalition** of 38 nations had

Great Britain's famed Desert Rats, members of the 7th Armored Brigade, were among coalition forces fighting the Iraqis.

11

banded together to fight Iraq. It included Arab countries such as Egypt and Syria. Even longtime enemies of the United States, such as the Soviet Union, supported the

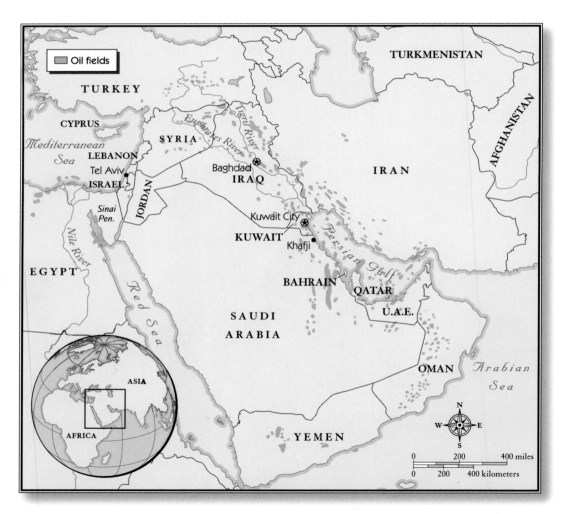

A map of the Middle East

allied coalition. The coalition's goal would be to drive Iraq's army from Kuwait.

The first step for the coalition was keeping the Iraqi army out of Saudi Arabia. The coalition forces gave their defensive campaign the code name Operation Desert Shield. Next, they set up a naval **blockade** of Iraq. To punish Iraq, the blockade stopped Iraqi ships from trading with other countries. The United Nations demanded that the Iraqi army leave Kuwait by January 15, 1991. If the soldiers refused, the coalition led by the United States would force them out.

As the deadline approached, U.S. President Bush sent Secretary of State James Baker to meet with Iraqi foreign minister Tariq Aziz. Baker told Aziz that Iraq had to leave Kuwait. Saddam Hussein refused to give in, however. Instead, he ruled Kuwait as brutally as he ruled Iraq. His soldiers arrested and tortured Kuwaiti civilians, stole money from Kuwait's banks, and stole valuable items from the national museum. Hussein **detained**

13

Saddam Hussein ruled Iraq as a cruel dictator.

thousands of people from the United States, Great Britain, and other countries who were living in Kuwait. He refused to let them go home and threatened to use them as human shields in case of an attack.

Hussein believed that the United States would not follow through on its threats of war. He believed that the American people would not support a war that might result in the loss of many American lives. Indeed, many Americans did not want the United States to take military action. On January 12, however, the U.S. Congress

14

voted to support a war against Iraq. The January 15 deadline came and went, and the Iraqi army remained in Kuwait. President Bush ordered coalition troops into war.

Members of the 101st Airborne Division march to a plane that will carry them to war.

DESERT STORM

Iraq appeared to be a fearsome foe. Its air force flew advanced fighter planes purchased from France and the Soviet Union. Its huge army had been tested by the long war with Iran. Iraq owned missiles called SCUDs that could be fired from mobile launchers and could travel hundreds of miles.

Saddam Hussein had proved willing to use any weapons available to defeat his enemies. Against Iran,

A Kurdish boy lived at a refuge camp in Turkey after fleeing Iraqi mustard gas attacks.

his troops had released poison gas. To put down a rebellion by Iraq's long-suffering Kurdish population, Hussein used deadly mustard gas. It killed hundreds of Kurds. No one knew if he would use similar weapons against coalition forces.

The coalition led by the United States had 670,000 troops, 200 warships, and thousands of attack helicopters, bomber aircraft, and fighter planes. The commander of this huge force was American General H. Norman Schwarzkopf. He launched a monthlong air attack that was named Operation Desert Storm.

U.S. Marine Corps jet fighters fly in formation during the Persian Gulf War.

17

The coalition's first targets were command centers in Iraq. The first shots of the war were fired by American Apache helicopters. They fired missiles at an Iraqi radar station, crippling Iraq's early warning system. The Persian Gulf War was on. "We will not fail," President Bush told the American people in a televised speech.

On January 17, the coalition began the precision bombing of selective targets in Iraq's capital, Baghdad.

Reporters from ABC, CNN, and other television networks reported live from Baghdad as the bombs began falling. Television cameras captured images of bright flashes and explosions lighting the night sky over Iraq. "An attack is under way," exclaimed ABC's Gary Shepard to millions of Americans watching on television.

That night, American bombers and missiles destroyed Iraqi communications centers and military headquarters. For the first time, the United States used large numbers of precision missiles fired from hundreds of miles away to strike targets. More than 200 targets in Iraq were hit on the

18

Coalition forces bombed Baghdad at night, leaving trails of light.

first night of bombing. Coalition air attacks continued to
pound Iraq for the next several weeks.

Saddam Hussein struck back. "The great showdown
has begun," he announced on Iraqi television. "The mother
of all battles is under way." Hussein ordered SCUD missiles

19

fired at Israel's largest city, Tel Aviv. Israel was the long-time enemy of Arab countries and the ally of the United States. Hussein hoped to provoke Israel into attacking Iraq. He believed that Arab nations would then leave the coalition and fight on Iraq's side against Israel.

His plan failed. The United States asked Israel not to respond to the attacks, and instead leave the defense of Israel to coalition forces. Most of Iraq's SCUDs missed their targets.

Hussein searched for other ways to fight back. On January 24, Iraqi troops released oil into the Persian Gulf off Kuwait. Over the next few days, an enormous **oil slick** grew in the water. It badly damaged the Persian Gulf environment and threatened the safety of Saudi drinking water.

On January 28, Hussein ordered an even bolder move. He sent his troops into Saudi Arabia for the first time. He hoped to capture some coalition forces and use them to force an end to the bombing campaign. He also

Iraqi SCUD missiles severely damaged buildings in Tel Aviv, Israel.

21

U.S. soldiers arrive at a burning oil refinery in Khafji after it was attacked by Iraqi forces.

hoped to inflict large numbers of U.S. casualties so
Americans at home would demand an end to the attacks.
The Iraqis captured the Saudi town of Khafji, but couldn't
hold the town for long. Two days later, Saudi troops
backed by American artillery pushed the Iraqis out.

22

Hussein's plans failed. It would be the only Iraqi ground attack of the war.

The coalition air attacks went on, and Iraq was nearly powerless to stop them. The coalition forces were using highly advanced weapons called smart weapons. Guided by lasers and complex electronics, these weapons could be aimed to strike a particular building from thousands of miles away. The air campaign was one of the most

A missile is launched toward Iraq from the USS Mississippi *Navy cruiser during Operation Desert Storm.*

23

intense in the history of war. Even smart weapons did not always work perfectly, however. Although they were aimed at Iraq's military, they sometimes struck and killed Iraqi civilians. On February 13, two American planes dropped bombs on an underground **bunker** in Baghdad. The United States believed the bunker was a military command center. The bunker also turned out to be a bomb shelter for civilians. At least 200 Iraqi civilians were killed, including women and children.

The air campaign against Iraq lasted for 37 days. It destroyed bridges, roads, airports, water treatment plants, and electrical power stations. Much of Iraq was in ruins. Thousands of Iraqi soldiers were dead. General Schwarzkopf said that the Iraqi military "was on the verge of collapse."

Still, Iraq's army continued its hold on Kuwait. On February 15, President Bush called on Iraqis to rise up against their leader. "There is another way for this

24

A bridge in Baghdad was destroyed during the air campaign against Iraq.

bloodshed to stop," he said, "and that is for the Iraqi military and the Iraqi people to take matters into their own hands and force Saddam Hussein, the dictator, to step aside."

THE GROUND WAR

On February 23, President Bush ordered coalition troops and tanks to advance through the desert. After 37 days of air warfare, the war on the ground was beginning. The Iraqis did all they could to prepare for the attack. In all, Iraq had about 400,000 soldiers ready for battle. Saddam Hussein hoped to depend on his trusted Republican Guard troops, the best in the Iraqi army. They planted thousands of land mines that would explode when tanks or troops passed over them. They dug trenches and built barriers of barbed wire to stop coalition troops. Coalition commanders also worried that Iraq would use poison gas or chemical weapons against their troops. They prepared themselves for a bloody and terrible fight.

Instead, the first wave of U.S. attackers smashed through the Iraqi defenses. The weeks of bombing had

An Egyptian light armored vehicle explodes after driving over an Iraqi mine.

left the Iraqis with no will to fight. Iraqi troops surrendered by the thousands. On the first day of the attack, more than 5,000 Iraqi soldiers were captured, and thousands more deserted. Hundreds of Iraqi tanks were

Iraqi troops surrendered to coalition forces in huge numbers.

destroyed. What was left of the Iraqi army retreated, and U.S. and other coalition forces poured into Kuwait.

All the Iraqis could do was launch more SCUD missiles. One hit a U.S. military barracks in Saudi Arabia.

28

It killed 28 soldiers and wounded 98 more. Still, the U.S.-led attack drove forward, pushing the Iraqi army out of Kuwait. As they retreated, the Iraqis set fire to more than 600 Kuwaiti oil wells. They also set fire to buildings and killed Kuwaiti civilians. Many Iraqi troops fled Kuwait in

A U.S. soldier stands atop a destroyed Iraqi tank as oil wells burn in the distance.

The road leading out of Kuwait became known as the Highway of Death.

stolen cars. They carried loads of stereos, clothes, furniture, and anything else they could steal.

U.S. forces chased the Iraqis as they fled Kuwait. U.S. warplanes flew over the crowded roads leading from Kuwait into Iraq and bombed the retreating Iraqi columns. The destruction was so complete that the road became known as the Highway of Death.

On February 26, coalition forces entered Kuwait City. The next day, the Kuwaiti flag was raised once more over the capital city. However, the fight was not over. Most of all, American commanders wanted to trap Iraq's elite Republican Guard. The Republican Guard was one of the keys to Saddam Hussein's power. If the guard could be destroyed, Hussein himself might topple from power. A part of the Republican Guard was crushed in a fierce tank battle on February 26. Much of the force, however, was able to escape into Iraq.

President Bush ordered a cease-fire, or a stop to the fighting, to take effect at 8 a.m. February 28.

A smiling Kuwaiti soldier raises the Kuwaiti flag.

"Kuwait is liberated," Bush told the American people. "Iraq's army is defeated." The United States and its coalition partners had sent almost 800,000 troops to fight Iraq. More than 500,000 of those troops were Americans.

One hundred forty-eight U.S. troops died in battle. Another 145 troops died in accidents or in other noncombat situations, and 467 were wounded in battle. (Later, many coalition soldiers claimed to suffer from a mysterious illness caused by their service in the war. The illness came to be called

A young girl, whose father died of suspected Gulf War Syndrome, attended a memorial service honoring England's war veterans in 2001.

Gulf War Syndrome. Experts disagreed about the nature and causes of the illness.)

No one knows exactly how many Iraqis died in the war. One estimate is that about 22,000 Iraqi soldiers and another 2,000 civilians were killed.

On March 3, General Schwarzkopf met with Iraq's generals to negotiate a formal end to the war. Iraq would

33

General H. Norman Schwarzkopf salutes an Iraqi general at the end of their negotiations.

have to release all coalition prisoners of war, pay Kuwait for the damage done during the war, and turn over any chemical and nuclear weapons. Schwarzkopf made one concession to the Iraqis. He agreed to let Iraq's army use helicopters to move its troops.

In southern Iraq, a rebellion against Saddam Hussein broke out. Ordinary Iraqis took up arms against his dictatorship. The revolt quickly spread to other parts of the country. Northern Iraq was home to millions of Kurdish people who had long suffered under Hussein's rule. They hoped that the war had weakened Hussein so badly that they could overthrow him. Earlier, President Bush had urged Iraqis to revolt. Iraqis hoped this meant that the United States would support their rebellions.

34

However, the United States decided not to intervene in the Iraqi civil war. Hussein and his army were free to use their attack helicopters to crush the rebellions. Up to 2 million Kurds left their homes to escape the fury of Hussein's power. They were forced to live in the mountains of northern Iraq with little food or fresh water. The United States and other countries sent food and medical supplies to help them survive, but no military support. It was a disheartening end to the war.

Kurdish rebels stand next to a defaced poster of Saddam Hussein during fighting in northern Iraq.

AFTER THE WAR

By April, all coalition prisoners had been released, and the official document ending the war was signed on April 6, 1991. Troops returned to the United States to a hero's welcome.

A young spectator holds a newspaper aloft during a victory parade in Washington, D.C.

Victory parades celebrated their return. There was good reason to celebrate. Saddam Hussein's invasion had been turned back. His huge army had been beaten. The United States had organized a vast coalition and sent its soldiers halfway around the world to fight. In a matter of weeks, those troops had won a crushing victory. They suffered very few casualties.

However, the war created enormous suffering. Thousands of civilians were killed by attacks from both sides. Between 2 million to 3 million Kuwaitis and Iraqis had to leave their homes and live as refugees. The roads, bridges, and buildings of Kuwait and Iraq had been damaged or destroyed. Entire towns would have to be rebuilt. Oil spills and oil fires had damaged the environment of the Persian Gulf region.

A Kurdish child cries out in despair at a Turkish refugee camp.

An Iraqi soldier keeps a close eye on UN weapons inspectors in Baghdad.

Most disturbing of all, Saddam Hussein remained in power. He ruled Iraq as brutally as he had before the war. Using what remained of his army, he suppressed revolts. Eventually, he broke promises made at the end of the war and refused to cooperate with inspectors from the United Nations looking for weapons of mass destruction.

As a result, coalition partners kept striking back at Iraq. The United States and Great Britain found a way to protect Iraq's Kurds from Hussein's army. They established a "no-fly zone" over northern Iraq, where Iraqi aircraft were not allowed to fly. To keep Iraqi aircraft out, U.S. and British planes patrolled the zone. Over the next decade, U.S. and British bombing raids on Iraq were frequent. In 1993, President Bill Clinton ordered

A U.S. F-16 jet patrols the "no-fly zone" over northern Iraq.

39

missiles fired at Iraqi military headquarters in Baghdad. The attack was in response to a plan by Iraq to kill former President Bush.

The United Nations tried to punish Iraq for not working with its weapons inspectors. It imposed economic **sanctions** on Iraq. These sanctions cut off Iraqi trade with other countries. Their aim was to weaken Saddam Hussein's rule and to drive him from power. Instead, the sanctions hurt ordinary Iraqi people, and Hussein stayed in power.

Saddam Hussein had survived the Persian Gulf War. He had survived a decade's worth of pressure from other countries that wanted him out of power. His regime could not survive another all-out war, however. In 2003, the United States launched another war against Iraq. President George W. Bush, the son of the former president, was convinced that Saddam Hussein had weapons of mass destruction and was building more.

In March 2003, the United States and Great Britain invaded Iraq. Saddam Hussein was finally forced out of power. His brutal reign was over, but life in Iraq remained difficult and unsettled.

An American soldier guards an area of downtown Baghdad in April 2003 following the U.S.-led invasion of Iraq.

41

GLOSSARY

blockade—the use of warships to shut down trade or communication with a port or ports

bunker—a strongly built room or building set beneath the ground to offer protection during war

coalition—union; alliance

detained—held prisoner

dictator—a ruler who takes complete control of a country, often unjustly

oil slick—a stain left on a body of water because of spilled oil

sanctions—punishments imposed to force a country to comply with certain laws

DID YOU KNOW?

- The oil well fires in Kuwait were put out by a crew of 200 firefighters from around the world. They came from Canada, China, Great Britain, France, Hungary, Iran, Kuwait, Romania, the Soviet Union, and the United States.

- Kuwait gained independence from Great Britain in 1961 and joined the United Nations in 1963.

IMPORTANT DATES

Timeline

1979	Saddam Hussein becomes president of Iraq.
1980	Hussein launches an eight-year war with Iran.
1990	Iraq invades Kuwait on August 2; President George H. W. Bush vows, "This will not stand."
1991	United States leads coalition of nations to drive Iraq from Kuwait.
1993	U.S. fires missiles at military headquarters in Iraq in response to hostile Iraqi actions.
2003	The United States and Great Britain invade Iraq; Saddam Hussein is forced out of power.

IMPORTANT PEOPLE

TARIQ AZIZ (1936–)
Iraqi foreign minister during the Persian Gulf War; later deputy foreign minister who surrendered to U.S. forces in July 2003

GEORGE H. W. BUSH (1924–)
President of the United States from 1989 to 1993

DICK CHENEY (1941–)
Secretary of defense during the administration of George H. W. Bush; elected vice president in 2000

SADDAM HUSSEIN (1937–)
Dictator of Iraq from 1979 until 2003, when his regime was overthrown

JABER AL-AHMAD AL SABAH (1928–)
Emir (royal ruler) of Kuwait since 1977

GENERAL H. NORMAN SCHWARZKOPF (1934–)
Commander in chief of the U.S. Central Command during the Persian Gulf War; retired from the military in August 1991

WANT TO KNOW MORE?

At the Library

Chant, Christopher. *The Gulf War.* New York: Marshall Cavendish, 1992.

Kent, Zachary. *The Persian Gulf War: The Mother of All Battles.* Hillside, N.J.: Enslow, 1994.

Nardo, Don. *The War Against Iraq.* San Diego, Calif.: Lucent Books, 2001.

On the Web

For more information on the *Persian Gulf War,* use

FactHound to track down Web sites related to this book.

1. Go to *www.compasspointbooks.com/facthound*

2. Type in this book ID: 0756506123

3. Click on the *Fetch It* button.

Your trusty FactHound will fetch the best Web sites for you!

Through the Mail

National Museum of Naval Aviation

1750 Radford Blvd.

Pensacola, Florida 32508

For information on one of the world's largest air and space museums

On the Road

United States Air Force Museum

Wright-Patterson Air Force Base

Dayton, Ohio 45433-7102

937/255-3284

To visit the largest military aviation museum in the world

INDEX

About the Author

Andrew Santella writes for magazines and newspapers, including GQ and the New York Times Book Review. He is the author of a number of books for young readers. He lives outside Chicago with his wife and son.